MW01282295

The Massachusetts OUI Survival Guide

A Step-By-By Guide To Defending Against Your Charges And Getting Your Life Back

First Edition

James M. Milligan Jr.
Law Office of James M. Milligan, Jr.

Table of Contents

Attorney James M. Milligan

Introduction

"The thing that is really hard,
and really amazing, is giving up
on being perfect and beginning
the work of becoming yourself."

– Anna Quindlen

We all make mistakes, but the consequences of these mistakes can vary dramatically depending on context. According to the most recent U.S. National Highway Traffic Safety Administration (NHTSA) poll on public attitudes about drinking and driving, one in five Americans admitted to driving while under the influence in the previous year. Two-thirds of those polled claimed to have done so in the previous month, suggesting that those who drink and drive do so regularly.

Although this is not to excuse the gravity of the offense, the data further suggest that being charged with an OUI or DUI results from a combination of *doing the wrong thing* and *having bad luck*. On a positive note, an OUI/DUI charge can be a wake-up call that starts you out on a path to becoming a better driver and a better person overall.

To regain a sense of empowerment and a positive outlook after an OUI/DUI charge, you need a better understanding of your rights and opportunities at each step of the way. That's why we put together this book for those who find themselves in the whirlwind of this legal process. In just a few short, simple chapters, you'll get the clarity you need to reclaim control. Here's what we'll be covering.

Section 1: Triage After Your OUI—The First Week

Although you can't change the past, you can commit to making better decisions and moving forward with confidence from the moment after your arrest. In this chapter, we'll discuss what you should do within the first few hours through the first few days after your

OUI arrest to minimize negative consequences. We'll discuss key points of Massachusetts state law; how to contest your driver's license suspension; and how to preserve evidence and witness testimony from the scene to substantiate your defense.

We'll also discuss how you can "triage your life" in the wake of the OUI, including how to manage work-related responsibilities, strategically break the news to your family, and secure adequate child care if necessary. You will also discover how to vet prospective attorneys and find an appropriate lawyer for your case, touching on the advantages of hiring a Board Certified Specialist in DUI/OUI Defense Law.

Section 2: The Nuts and Bolts of OUI Defense

Some of the subjects we will touch upon in this section include:

- The trial preparation and discovery process.

- Contingencies and defense options for first, second, third or fourth OUI offenses.

- Sentencing standards and your alternative options.

- The kinds of evidence that can be used against you, such as Field Sobriety Tests (FSTs), blood tests, breath tests, and police testimony.

- Specific case laws (e.g. <u>Commonwealth v. Zeininger, 459 mass. 775 (2011),</u> and legal strategies for challenging each type of evidence.

- How to minimize insurance rate spikes after your OUI or how to deal with insurance companies if you have been involved in an accident.

Section 3: Getting Your Life Back in Order After Your OUI Defense

This section will cover non-legal issues that arise in the aftermath of an OUI charge. We'll touch on how to keep your job and/or stay in school despite the charges and answer diverse, pressing questions, such as:

- *How should I talk about the OUI and subsequent penalties to important people in my life?*

- *How will I get around on a daily basis if my driver's license is suspended?*

- *Where can I turn to get help for a drug and/or alcohol problem?*

- *What positive life changes can I make to cope more effectively with day-to-day challenges?*

Section 4: Resources and Conclusion

Finally, we include a short compendium of local resources for OUI offenders in Massachusetts, including Alcoholics Anonymous and Massachusetts state certified OUI programs

If you have additional questions or concerns at any time, please reach out to the team at the Law Office of James M. Milligan, Jr. for a private case evaluation at (888) 684-6494.

Triage After Your OUI—
The First Week

"Yesterday is gone. Tomorrow
has not yet come. We have
only today. Let us begin."

— Mother Teresa

The initial aftermath of an OUI arrest is often disorienting and surreal. One minute you're enjoying yourself at the bar with friends and loved ones, and the next you're in police custody, facing the life-changing prospect of an OUI charge. It's natural, and even potentially self-motivating, to feel regret and remorse for your decision to get behind the wheel while under the influence or perhaps you were responsible in your drinking and got arrested anyway. In any event, you need to know your rights and options before just accepting any and all penalties for what happened. There are many far reaching effects an OUI can have on your life aside from the penalties the court may impose, and it is important to have all the cards on the table before making any decisions on how best to handle your case.

The Facts About License Suspensions

If you refused to take a breath test, your license will be suspended for a minimum of 180 days up to life depending on how many prior OUI offenses you have on your record. Massachusetts has a lifetime lookback period, so no matter how far back your prior OUI offense was, it is taken into account. Additionally, any OUI offense in another state will most likely count as a prior OUI offense, even if you received a lesser offense in that state. For instance, some states have a Driving While Ability Impaired. If on the other hand, your prior OUI was reduced to a Reckless or Negligent Operation of a motor vehicle this would not qualify as a prior OUI.

According to Massachusetts General Laws, you may request a hearing within 15 days after the police confiscate your license. At this hearing, you will have to provide proof for one of the following defenses:

- It was not reasonable for the officer to suspect you were intoxicated.

- You were never placed under arrest.

- You actually consented to the blood or breath test requested.

If you provide a convincing defense, the suspension will be lifted, and your license will be deemed valid again. There is no hardship eligibility on a refusal suspension with one exception; first time offenders who are willing to take a plea deal and enroll in an alcohol program are eligible to apply for a hardship license through the Registry of Motor Vehicles. The hardship license is a 12 hour license for 7 days a week and can be used for any purpose once it is issued.

If you are later convicted or admit to an OUI, your license will be suspended again for an additional 45 days to life, depending on your prior OUI history. The refusal and conviction suspensions run consecutively and not concurrently. For instance, if you are a first offender and refuse to take a breath test, the total license suspension if you plead or are found Guilty after trial would be 180+45-90 days. Under this scenario, you would be eligible for a hardship license.

Collecting Evidence

The earlier you gather evidence, the better, because your attorney can use this information to test or refute assumptions about what happened and what the police did or did not do. For instance, let's say you failed a breathalyzer test — that is, the test seemed to show that you were under the influence. Many factors could have created what's called a "false positive," such as:

- The presence of "mouth alcohol" from recently-consumed drinks, mouthwash, medication, and other substances.

- Improper calibration of the breathalyzer device.

- Biological processes during the absorption phase.

- Software glitches and other technology errors.

- Human error through improper usage, application, and interpretation of the breathalyzer equipment and results.

For example, let's say you submitted to a breathalyzer test that resulted in a seemingly implausible .08 percent blood alcohol content (BAC) reading. However, acting quickly but carefully, you do the following. You obtain a detailed copy of your receipt from the bar you patronized on the night of the incident; collect security footage from cameras surrounding the venue, and get witness testimony from your server.

Bear in mind that time will be of the essence, since evidence can be lost or degraded, and witness testimony tends to become forgotten/distorted if not recorded soon after an event.

The receipt could demonstrate that you purchased one alcoholic beverage at 8:00PM, while your server and/or security camera footage could testify to the fact that you finished the drink and left the establishment at 8:15PM. If the police report indicates that the breathalyzer test was administered at 9:00 PM, you could make a fairly strong case that it is inconceivable from a toxicology standpoint that your blood alcohol level was that high. The general rule of thumb is that one beer, shot of alcohol or 8 oz glass of wine will result in a .025 blood alcohol level in the body.

Nailing Down the Details

As just mentioned, countless studies have shown that human memory becomes increasingly less reliable as time passes. To ensure an accurate accounting of every detail, and to prevent potential inconsistencies in your defense, write down as much as possible about the events leading up to your arrest. Consider the following best practices:

- Establish a precise timeline by referring to receipts, text messages, and other time-stamped records.

- Take down witness statements from your vehicle passengers, your bartender that evening, citizens at the scene of the accident, etc.

- Undergo an extensive medical evaluation to document your current health and determine the potential influence of certain conditions and/or medications.

- Take videos and photographs at the scene of the accident, and track down security camera footage and/or footage from traffic light cameras.

- Perhaps you have photos from the evening that show you look fine.

It may be tempting to skip the details, especially if you're feeling overwhelmed or defeated. "What does

JAMES M. MILLIGAN JR.

it matter?" you might think. "The cops already have what they need."

Remember that in an OUI case, the prosecution is required to prove *every element* of the OUI charge beyond a reasonable doubt, this is the highest legal standard in any criminal justice system in the world. If the prosecution cannot prove even one element beyond a reasonable doubt, you cannot be convicted of the charge. Items like timelines, witness statements, medical records, and photographs pin down the details, making it more likely that "reasonable doubt" will continue to exist even when the prosecution has said all they can say. When it comes to defending yourself in an OUI case, the details matter.

Seeking Medical Treatment

There are two reasons to seek medical treatment after an OUI arrest:

1. To establish your existing state of health and to review your current medical conditions, daily medications, and other factors

to determine whether any of them may have influenced your case,

2. To treat any injuries, you may have suffered as a result of an accident or the OUI arrest process itself.

If your OUI involved a car accident, a medical examination is a must even if you felt fine after the accident; often times concussion symptoms and injuries are not felt until hours after an accident. Even if there was no crash, however, it is important to see a doctor as soon as possible. During your appointment, you may wish to discuss the following issues:

- **Current diagnoses and medical conditions.** What conditions, if any, do you already have? Are they well-managed with your current treatment plan? How often do you see a doctor for them? When you see a doctor after your OUI, talk about these conditions and how they might interact with alcohol or other substances.

- **Current medications.** Many prescription medications can interact with alcohol in ways that produce symptoms similar to intoxication, even though your mind and reflexes remain alert. Some of these effects can linger even after the active portion of the medication is out of your system. Review your current medications with your doctor or pharmacist. In looking at medications and possible interaction with alcohol, you need to be careful because if combined with alcohol they may exacerbate the effect of the alcohol, thus making you impaired even though you did not consume a lot of alcohol. That is to say that alcohol does not need to be the only cause of impairment. See <u>Commonwealth v. Stathopoulos</u>, 401 Mass. 453 (1988) (Combined effects of alcohol and illicit drugs rendered the defendant under the influence of alcohol).

- There is a distinction to be made between prescription medication taken responsibly and illicit drugs or prescription medication that is abused. The situation, where both alcohol and illegal drugs are concurrent causes of the defendant's voluntary intoxication, must be distinguished from that where a legally prescribed drug may have been the cause of the defendant's involuntary intoxication. "[Where a defendant suffers intoxicating effects from prescription medication used as instructed . . . , if the defendant had reason to know that her use of alcohol might combine with her prescription medications to impair her mental faculties, and such a combined effect was in fact the cause of her diminished abilities, she would be deemed criminally responsible for her actions. If, on the other hand, she had no such foreknowledge, or if her mental defect existed wholly apart from any use of alcohol, the defense [of involuntary intoxication] would be available . . . . [T]he Commonwealth bears the burden of proving that the defendant's intoxication was voluntary." Commonwealth v. Darch, 54 Mass. App. Ct. 713, 715-716 (2002).

- **Any undiagnosed conditions or new symptoms.** If you are having new or unusual symptoms, or symptoms of something that has not yet been diagnosed, don't forget to mention these as well. In some cases, the OUI can lead to a diagnosis that would not have been made otherwise.

If you've been injured during your OUI, your medical appointment should also focus on examining and treating your injuries. Be honest about the source of your injuries, but don't beat yourself up for them. Just stick to the facts. For instance, if the doctor asks what happened, explain: "I was in an accident. My car ran into a light pole." These facts help your physician focus on diagnosing and treating your injuries.

If you were taken into police custody as part of your arrest, you may have received some medical care from emergency medical personnel or from medical staff at the jail. While these can be first steps toward care, seeing your own doctor as soon as you can is essential. In most OUI cases, neither emergency medical personnel nor jail medical staff are focusing on a comprehensive examination. Their job is to find and treat immediate and potentially life-threatening conditions – not to think about the many ways in which your unique medical history might have affected your OUI case.

During your OUI defense, your attorney will likely seek certified copies of your medical records for use in court. These records can, and often do, play a crucial role in an OUI defense. Attorneys who are Board Certified Specialists in DUI defense law understand the particular importance medical records can play.

I was assaulted during the events that led to my arrest. What medical care do I need?

In some cases, OUI arrests follow another event, like a fight or assault. While obtaining medical care, be sure to mention the fact that you were assaulted to the paramedics, doctors, and other medical professionals who treat you for your injuries. You will both preserve evidence for your own potential OUI case and help establish any claim you have against the person who attacked you.

What about blood tests?

In Massachusetts, police cannot take your blood unless you have been arrested and consent to a blood test. Otherwise, breath testing is the only option available for police to test your blood alcohol concentration at the scene.

Despite this rule, many police pressure injured people to submit to blood tests, and many people give in because they are not familiar with the rules. If you were forced to undergo a blood alcohol test, your lawyer can help ensure that any testing that violated your rights is suppressed and excluded from use at a trial.

Triage Your Life: The First Week After Your OUI

An OUI arrest has far-reaching consequences, even if you did nothing wrong. During the first week following your OUI, you'll need to address potential problems in many areas of your life. These include:

- **Work.** An OUI can complicate your work in many ways. We'll discuss how to minimize the damage.

- **Telling your family.** Breaking the news to your family, friends, or roommates is never easy. Here are some tips.

- **Child care.** Finding child care can be tough after an OUI – and if you work with children, you may have even more trouble.

An arrest or charge is not the same as a conviction. Unfortunately, an arrest or charge can be enough to affect your professional credentials in some fields – and it can certainly affect how bosses, family, and friends view you.

Do I have to tell my boss about my OUI?

The answer is "it depends." Generally speaking, you do not have to tell anyone about your OUI arrest or charge. Anyone can be accused of a crime, and a charge does not prove that you are guilty. Since an accusation can make you look bad, it is best to keep that accusation to yourself when you are able.

Realize, however, that you cannot always keep an OUI arrest or charge to yourself – even at work.

Generally speaking, you should disclose your OUI arrest or charge if:

1. **Your contract or employee handbook requires you to do so.** If you have a work contract, and it requires you to report arrests or criminal charges, tell your employer. If you don't disclose, you could be fired for breaching your employment contract or violating company policies, even if you are never convicted.

2. **Your job requires you to drive.** An OUI arrest or charge may affect your ability to do your job, particularly if you are without a driver's license. Your employer may also choose to assign you to other duties until the case is resolved, in order to protect itself from liability.

3. **Your boss asks you directly.** If you are asked point-blank, do not lie. Your boss may or may not fire you for the OUI, but many employers will fire you for lying about one.

Licensed professionals – including doctors, nurses, pharmacists, lawyers, and many others - may be required by their licensing authorities to report an OUI arrest, charge, or conviction. However, you may be required to tell the licensing board directly, rather than your employer. Check *both* your employee handbook, policies, or contract *and* your licensing body's rules to determine who must be told.

Look carefully! Some employers require you to report any arrest, charge, or license suspension. Others only require you to report if you are actually convicted of a crime. Make sure you know what you have to share before you talk to your employer.

When you speak to your employer:

Keep these tips in mind.

1. **Stick to the facts.** A good formula to use is the important fact, followed by why you are saying it. For example, if your labor contract requires you to disclose a criminal charge, you might say "I was arrested

and charged with an OUI this past week-end. I am reporting this because our labor contract requires me to report any criminal charges against me." Or if you are reporting it because you drive as part of your job, you might say "I am reporting this because my driver's license has been suspended."

2. **Provide any information you have in your favor.** For example, suppose you are talking to your boss on a Monday morning because your license has been suspended. Inform your employer that you cannot drive today, but you expect to learn more about when you can get your license restored after speaking with your OUI lawyer. Reporting this helps your employer plan and demon-strates that you are taking proactive steps to prevent the OUI charges from affecting your work.

3. **Don't make excuses.** One of the ways an arrest or charge can make you look bad is by putting you in a position where you feel you

have to make excuses – which can make you look like you have something to hide. Resist the urge to talk about the arrest itself. If your employer asks what happened, simply say, "I have an attorney (or "I'm looking for an attorney"), and we are working on it." If you want, you can apologize for the inconvenience the charges may have caused your employer – but don't apologize for the arrest itself. You are innocent until proven guilty in court.

I'm applying for jobs. Do I have to disclose my OUI arrest or charge?

Read the applications carefully. If the question asks, "Have you ever been arrested?" you'll have to answer yes. If the application asks if you've ever been convicted, you don't have to mention your current OUI unless you are found guilty. You do, however, have to mention any prior convictions that you have.

Also, remember that in most cases in Massachusetts, an OUI is a misdemeanor. If a job application asks about both misdemeanor and felony arrests, you'll have to answer yes. But if it asks only about felony arrests or convictions, you do not have to mention any misdemeanors – including most OUIs. An OUI becomes a felony if you have been convicted of a third offense.

Telling the Family

Your family, friends, and loved ones share considerable time with you. Sooner or later, they are going to realize that something is on your mind. Your family or roommate may notice that you are not driving, that you have been researching board-certified OUI defense lawyers online, or that you are spending considerable time outside the house.

It is important to tell those closest to you about your OUI arrest or charge. The longer you wait, the more likely they are to feel betrayed. Although telling them feels unpleasant, they can be an important source of support and comfort during this difficult process.

There is no one "right" way to tell your family and loved ones. Instead, keep these guidelines in mind as you decide who to tell, when to tell them, and what to say.

1. **Start with the facts.** The easiest way to start the conversation is with the facts of what happened: "I was arrested last weekend and charged with an OUI."

2. **Be emotionally prepared.** Many people don't know how to respond to the news that a loved one is facing an OUI charge so be prepared for anything. For the most part though your loved ones will always support you despite being disappointed or upset.

3. **Remember that the first response is not always the last.** If your loved one responds negatively, remember that they may have a different response once they have a chance to process their feelings and think about the situation. It is okay to walk away temporarily to allow both yourself and others to process the information.

4. **Share the next steps, if you know them.** For instance, if you have a hearing to restore your driver's license coming up, mention the hearing and the date. If you have found a lawyer you trust, talk about this step as well.

5. **Consider talking to a lawyer before you talk to your family.** By talking to a lawyer you trust, you can learn more about the next steps in your case. Sharing this information with your family helps to empower them, which can provide a sense of comfort and control – which they can then use to help you.

What about the kids?

Kids are perceptive. They notice when something is going on in the house. When they are not told what's happening, they may jump to dire conclusions, which can negatively affect their schoolwork, play, and friendships.

You now your children better than anyone. Depending on their age it might be best to tell your children about your OUI arrest or charges yourself. You do not want them to read about it in the local paper or hear it from other kids on the playground. For those parents with high school/college aged children, this might be an opportunity to warn them about the dangers of drinking and driving and stress the importance of being responsible.

When talking to your kids about an OUI, put the facts in words they can understand. Answer their questions honestly, but don't "overload" them. For instance, you might talk about what step you will take next, but don't explain what *might* happen unless they ask. Reassure them that you will do everything you can to ensure that their lives continue normally, and that you still love them, no matter what happens.

Kids don't always express negative emotions in the same way adults do. Instead of yelling, for instance, your child may become withdrawn or appear to lose interest in things they normally enjoy. It can take children much longer than adults to "work out" their feelings. Remind your kids that you (and other trusted adults) are available any time they want to talk.

You are not required to tell your child care provider about an OUI. However, you may face some difficulties getting your kids to daycare – or transporting them to school or after-school activities. Here are some steps that may help.

- **Ask a family member.** If you have already disclosed the OUI arrest or charge to a family member, he or she may be willing to transport the kids for a few days. It may help to remind family that this is favor they're doing for the children directly.

- **Look at carpool options.** Can the parent of another child transport your kids to school or activities? When asking, don't mention your OUI. Simply say that you need help for a few days, and that you'll be happy to return the favor when you are able.

- **Review the bus route.** Many families drive their kids to school instead of having them take the bus because it is convenient – for instance, the school is on the way to the parent's place of work. If your children have the option to take the school bus, use it. Also, check to see if the school has a "late bus" option that would allow children to stay for after-school activities and still find a ride home.

- **Break it to the children gently.** If all else fails, you may need to explain that the kids cannot go to a favorite activity for a few days. Tell them that you expect the break to be short, and plan a fun activity at home to keep them occupied.

Whatever you do, resist the urge to drive the kids yourself until your license is restored. Being caught driving on a suspended license with children in the vehicle can land you in additional trouble.

How to Find and Vet An Attorney

For many people, their OUI arrest or charge is their first experience with the police and courts. They do not have a lawyer of their own, and they have little experience in choosing the right lawyer for their case.

If this sounds familiar, here's how to find the right lawyer for you.

Where should I look?

Some of the most popular sources for finding an attorney include:

- **Online searches.** Using your favorite search engine will yield a wide range of results. To narrow down the options, consider adding search terms. A search string like "Massachusetts board certified OUI defense lawyer" will yield more focused, specific results than "defense lawyer" or "OUI lawyer." Some lawyers are very "tech" savy and know how to get to the top of any search engine inquiry but have little experience when it comes to OUI cases and/or have a questionable reputation.

- **Attorney ranking sites.** Martindale-Hubbell, Avvo, and similar websites gather information on lawyers, allowing you to search by location, practice area, certifications, and more. They also provide ratings and reviews, which can help you evaluate your options. Reviews from former clients can be very useful in the selection process.

- **Word of mouth.** Many lawyers build their practices on the positive referrals they get from former clients whose cases they have handled successfully. When relying on word of mouth, however, remember that every OUI case is different. Choose a lawyer who will look for the best course of action in *your* case.

Once you have narrowed down your options, it is time to start talking to the top choices on your list. Don't be afraid to ask questions. The best lawyers welcome questions as a sign that you have done your homework and are serious about winning your case.

Some key questions to ask prospective attorneys include:

- **Is the Lawyer a Board Certified OUI lawyer?** A Board Certified OUI Lawyer is someone who has taken a proficiency examination in all areas relating to an OUI practice and will be well suited to address any issues that arise in your case.

- **How many years have you been practicing OUI defense law?** It's important to ask not only how long a lawyer has practiced, but also how long they have focused on the area you need.

- **Has the Lawyer lectured or taught in the area of OUI law?** OUI lawyers that have been invited to speak or lecture on OUI topics generally have been asked because of their experience and reputation as one of the top lawyers in their field.

- **What kind of experience do you have handling a case like mine?** Choose a lawyer who convinces you that he or she has been down this road before and knows what to do.

- **How many cases have you taken to jury trial? What happened?** While some cases are resolved before trial, a trial is one option and a right. Make sure your lawyer can see a trial through to a successful conclusion.

- **Who in the office will be handling my case? What are their qualifications?** Most lawyers work with teams that include both other attorneys and non-lawyer professionals like paralegals. Make sure you know to whom you'll be talking and who will be doing most of the work. Every successful, accomplished OUI attorney has to rely on competent support staff and associate lawyers to assist them run their office.

- **What challenges do you see in my case?** Every case presents certain hurdles. The lawyer should be able to explain what these are and what they mean for your case in a way you understand.

- **How will you communicate with me about my case?** Make sure you are comfortable with the level of communication proposed.

- **What are the potential costs?** Choose a lawyer who explains costs and fees realistically. It is better to be prepared than to be surprised by a final bill that is much larger than expected. Criminal cases should be based upon flat fees, not on an hourly or per court appearance basis. Lawyers that bill in this way should be eliminated from your selection process because often times there are delays in the court that are not the result of the client and it seems unfair for the client to bear that cost.

These initial consultations are usually free, and they are always confidential. Their purpose is to help you decide if you want to work with this lawyer, and to help the lawyer decide how best to handle your case. The lawyer's role in this process is to lay the cards on the table, make some recommendations and then let you decide what is in your best interests based upon the information and facts that have been provided by the lawyer.

The Nuts and Bolts of OUI Defense

"The biggest risk is not taking any risk... In a world that's changing really quickly, the only strategy that is guaranteed to fail is not taking risks."

– Mark Zuckerberg

What does it take to successfully defend against an OUI charge?

In this section, we'll walk through the process of building and executing an OUI defense. We'll look at what will happen, why, and in what order. This section covers:

- Trial preparation, including the investigative process known as "discovery."

- Contingencies for 1st, 2nd, 3rd, and 4th OUIs and your options for each.

- Sentencing standards for OUI and alternative sentencing options.

- The evidence that may be used against you in an OUI case and how to address it.

- Key cases that govern OUI in Massachusetts and how to challenge them.

- How to handle important related matters, like getting your license reinstated and minimizing the impact on your insurance costs.

An OUI defense works best when you and your lawyer can work together. This section seeks to give you the information you need to be a strong partner in your own case.

Preparing for an OUI Trial: Meeting Your Lawyer

You've been arrested and charged with an OUI. You need a lawyer – fast. And you need to be ready to help your lawyer build a strong case on your behalf.

Be ready to talk about the following points during your first interview with your lawyer:

- **A detailed account of what happened.** Your lawyer will want every detail you can remember: times, places, distances, how you traveled, who you were with, what you did (or did not) drink. Many people find it helpful to start making a timeline before they meet with their lawyer, adding to it as they recall certain details.

- **A detailed medical background.** Be ready to talk about any physical injuries or conditions you have, any medications you take, and when you last saw a doctor. The way your body metabolizes alcohol or other substances is key to an OUI defense – and the answers can often be found in your medical history.

- **Your criminal background in Massachusetts or other states.** Have you been arrested, charged, or convicted of any crime in the past in any state? If so, it may affect your sentence if you are convicted in this case. Be straightforward about what happened and the sentence(s) you received.

- **A copy of your driving history.** The official Mass RMV website provides an unofficial copy of your history for $6 and will email it to you within minutes of the request. Your lawyer will almost certainly ask for one, so it makes sense to order it before your initial interview.

If you have any other paperwork related to your OUI arrest or charge, bring it with you. Notices relating to license suspension hearings, copies of police reports, or copies of hospital discharge paperwork all fall into this category.

Preparing for an OUI Trial: Discovery

"Discovery" is the formal process of gathering and sharing information. Both the prosecution and the defense participate in discovery in order to learn what the other side knows, gather information, and determine whether any issues can be resolved before trial.

Most board-certified OUI defense lawyers will include a set of standard steps in their discovery process. If it is available your lawyer will likely gather information like:

- **Medical records.** If you were injured or a blood test was performed, these records are more likely to be involved in your case.

- **Names, addresses, and dates of birth of witnesses.** These may include witnesses to your behavior before you got in the vehicle, witnesses to your driving, or witnesses who interacted with you during or after your arrest.

- **Maps or diagrams of the place the stop occurred.** Google Earth and Google Maps have made it easier than ever for lawyers to see the actual location of the stop that led to an arrest – which is a key point in many OUI cases.

- **Copies of the police officers' field sobriety test (FST) guidelines.** These are typically included in the standard manual given to all officers and troopers during their academy training. They play a crucial role in spotting ways in which a field sobriety test may be performed inaccurately, calling the results into question.

- **Copies of any receipts and/or videos.** In this day and age, most establishments have electronic receipts that can be obtained after the fact even if you did not keep the receipt or threw it away. Go back to the establishment and ask for a copy of the receipt and/or itemized bill. Moreover, almost every business has video camera surveillance. Take note of whether this technology exists at the business, and inform your lawyer, so they he/she can request that the video be preserved and get a court order to produce the video.

Your lawyer will ask you for any specific items you need to provide. For everything else, your attorney's office will take the lead on gathering the information.

Be prepared! Criminal trial rules in Massachusetts require both the prosecution and the defense to share information with one another. If one side does not provide discovery to the other, the information cannot be used at trial. Your lawyer is not trying to damage your case, but to ensure the best possible outcome.

In fact, because prosecutors work closely with police, this "sharing" requirement often plays out in favor of the defense. Police and prosecutors often have access to "exculpatory" evidence, or evidence that demonstrates that you are not guilty. Prior to the U.S. Supreme Court's ruling in *Brady v. Maryland*, 373 U.S. 83 (1963), police and prosecutors did not have to reveal this evidence to the defense. Today, they do.

How long does discovery take?

Discovery may take anywhere from a few weeks to a few months, depending on how complex your case is. Delays by the prosecution can also delay discovery. However, your lawyer can take steps to turn a delay to your advantage – for instance, by asking the court to exclude any discovery that has not been shared by the first trial date.

Preparing for an OUI Trial: Preparing Witnesses and Choosing the Jury

Before your trial date, you will meet with your lawyer again to talk about the trial itself. Your lawyer might also ask the witnesses in your favor to attend this meeting, so that they are ready as well. Key points that will be covered in this meeting include jury selection, the arguments to be made in your defense, and preparing the client and the witnesses to testify in support of those theories.

What arguments will be made? How will my lawyer back them up?

It always important to remember that it is the government's burden of proof to show that you are

Guilty beyond a reasonable doubt. The best arguments for your defense depend on the facts of your case. In many instances, there are no witnesses to call on your behalf or medical records and we are simply challenging whether the government can prove their case against you. Typically, defense arguments in an OUI case fall into one of two categories, pre trial motions and trial:

- **Your rights were violated.** Typically, these motions are done prior to your trial date. These arguments point to facts that show that the police or prosecution violated your Constitutional rights during your arrest, while gathering evidence, or while charging you with an OUI. Questions about how you were questioned, whether the proper warrant was obtained, or whether discovery was carried out correctly all fall in this category.

- **You didn't do it.** These arguments point to facts that show that you did not violate Massachusetts OUI law. Questions about your blood alcohol levels, behavior, performance on field sobriety tests and driving all fall in this category.

Both types of argument are typically supported in the same way during an OUI trial: with witness testimony, documentation (also known as "exhibits"), and arguments made by your lawyer.

How is the jury selected?

Jury selection is carried out through a process known as "voir dire." Prospective jurors will enter the courtroom, be sworn in, and be asked questions a series of questions to determine whether the jurors can be fair and impartial. Defense counsel will often request that the judge ask the jurors: 1) whether they are opposed to the use of alcohol, 2) whether they have any close relationship with law enforcement, that is, would they credit their testimony simply because they are police officers, 3) Are the jurors opposed to the use of alcohol for religious or moral reasons, and 4) has any of the jurors had any experience with OUI offenses. Each lawyer will then have the opportunity to strike a juror either "for cause," or to use a "peremptory" strike.

"For cause" strikes are used for jurors who are related to anyone involved in the case, have any financial or legal "stake" in the case, or have formed an opinion, bias, or prejudice prior to hearing the facts. "Peremptory" strikes can be used without explaining the cause. Each side gets a limited number of peremptory strikes depending on whether the case is in District Court or Superior Court.

Once both sides can agree on the jurors that are seated, those jurors are sworn in and given instructions as to their job: to hear the facts of your case and to decide whether the prosecution has proved every element of the charge beyond a reasonable doubt. In the District Court, it is a 6 person jury, and in the Superior Court it is a 12 person jury. Often times, we will impanel alternate jurors just in case one of the jurors needs to be excused.

What happens during a trial?

Criminal trials tend to follow a predictable pattern, which includes the following steps:

- **Jury selection.** The jurors are chosen, and the judge explains their job to them.

- **Preliminary matters or Motion in Limine.** One or both lawyers may wish to make a motion before the trial starts to limit or exclude certain evidence, or to handle other matters. These items are always heard outside the hearing of the jury either before the trial starts or at "side bar" which is a private conversation with the judge at his/her bench and the lawyers.

- **Opening statements.** The opening statement often marks the "formal" beginning of the trial. Each side has the chance to make an opening statement. In the statement, each party's lawyer points out the facts they intend to prove. It is essentially a "road map" of the evidence from both sides perspective.

- **Prosecution's case in chief.** The prosecution calls witnesses and provides evidence. Their goal is to prove every element of every charge you face beyond a reasonable doubt. The government will ask questions of their witnesses, called direct examination. Once direct testimony is done, the defense will then have an opportunity to question that witness, called cross-examination. This process will continue until the government has called all of their witnesses and "rests."

- **Defense's case in chief.** Once the prosecution "rests," or ends its case, it is the defense's turn. Some defense lawyers choose to give their opening statement here, instead of at the start of the trial. Your lawyer's goal is to demonstrate that reasonable doubt exists, or to prove any affirmative defenses beyond a reasonable doubt. Again, witnesses and evidence may used to achieve this goal. It always important to remember that it is the government's burden of proof to show that you are Guilty beyond a reasonable doubt. If the lawyers feels as though the government has failed to prove their case after calling their witnesses, then the lawyer may "rest" as well, even though you have witnesses or evidence to present.

- **Closing statements.** Once the defense "rests," both sides have the chance to make a closing statement. Unlike an opening statement, the purpose of a closing statement is to persuade the jury, not to state the facts. The defense lawyer's role is to argue the facts of the case referencing the jury instructions that will be provided to them by the judge.

- **Jury instructions.** The judge reads instructions to the jury that explain each charge and what the jury must consider in order to find the defendant guilty of that charge.

- **Jury deliberation.** The jury moves to the jury room to talk about the facts of the case and to reach a verdict. This process can take anywhere from a few minutes to several days, if the case is complex. A jury's verdict must be unanimous.

- **Verdict.** The jury returns to the courtroom and announces the verdict. If a "guilty" verdict is returned, the government will move for sentencing typically done on the same day as the trial.

- **Sentencing.** At sentencing, both lawyers argue for or against certain penalties. The judge hears these arguments and makes a decision. The judge may also decide to hear statements from you or from others involved in the case.

The length of each step depends on the complexity of the case, the number of objections raised, and other factors. Nonetheless, most OUI trials take only one or two days to complete.

Can I testify on my own behalf? Should I?

You have the right in any trial to testify on your own behalf. You also have the right *not* to do so. This is your right, and the government cannot force you to testify.

In an OUI case, your lawyer may recommend that you do not take the stand. The evidence can frequently be contested more effectively through questioning the method by which it was collected, pointing out that certain tests are not scientifically based, and examining the events leading up to the stop. If you take the stand, you run the risk of the prosecution twisting your words to make it sound like you did something that you did not do – or to make it sound like you are lying about the events of the evening. Instead of getting to tell your story, you may end up accidentally telling the story the prosecutor wants you to tell.

Some people choose to take the stand in their own OUI case and feel good about doing so. However, what worked for them may not work for you. The decision whether or not to testify on your own behalf must be made based on the facts of each individual case. Your lawyer will get you ready to testify, but prior to testifying you can assess how the government's case looks and then make the decision as to whether your testimony will help or hurt the case.

Contingencies and Options for OUI Charges

Massachusetts imposes an escalating series of penalties for first, second, third, and fourth OUI offenses.

The differing impacts of each charge mean that the options and the legal strategy for defending against each one change as well.

First Offense

A first OUI conviction in Massachusetts comes with penalties like:

- $500 to $1500 in fines,

- Up to 2 ½ years (30 months) in prison,

- 1 year driver's license suspension.

If you refused a breath test, your license will be suspended for 180 days. If you agreed to the breath test and blew above a .08, your license will be suspended for 30 days. If you choose the fight the case, you will get your license back after 30 days; or if your case is still pending after the 180 days, you will get your license back for a fee of $500 to the Registry of Motor Vehicles. If you fight the case, there is no hardship or temporary license during the 30 or 180 day suspension.

The standard disposition of a 1st OUI in Massachusetts includes items like:

- A Continuance Without a Finding (CWOF). This is not the same as a "guilty" conviction on your record as long as you follow all the terms and conditions.

- 1 year of probation.

- Approximately $1380 in fees and fines.

- 45 to 90 day drivers' license suspension (in addition to any other suspension)

- You are eligible for a 12-hour "hardship license" to allow limited driving privileges. Choose a lawyer who can help you fight for this option, as most lawyers will not assist you with this process.

- A 1 year suspension of your CDL, if you have one.

If you plead guilty without going to trial, these are the most likely consequences. If you decide to go to trial and win, you get your license back and keep the OUI off your criminal record. If you lose at trial, these are the most likely consequences – except that the OUI is more will be entered on your record as a Guilty (conviction) rather than as a CWOF.

Second Offense

A second OUI offense in Massachusetts comes with penalties like:

- $600 to $10,000 in fines,

- 30 days to 2 ½ years (30 months) in prison,

- 2 year driver's license suspension,

- An ignition interlock device placed on your vehicle.

If you refused to take a breath test, your license will be suspended for three years. If you took the breath test and blew a .08 or above, your license will be suspended for 30 days.

A conviction for a second OUI most often comes with these penalties:

- A guilty finding with probation,

- At least 60 days in jail (up to 2 years),

- $600 to $10,000 in fines,

- A 2 year license suspension, but you may be eligible for a work/education hardship exemption in 1 year. This is in addition to any other suspension you face. It is important to note that the 2 year suspension is consecutive to the 3 year refusal suspension. That is, the 3 year refusal suspension plus 2 years for the 2nd offense. You have to serve 1 year of the 2 year suspension. Essentially, you will not be eligible for a hardship license through the RMV for 4 years, although you may apply to the Board of Appeals sooner to request hardship relief. This gets confusing, so make sure you have a lawyer who can clearly communicate your license options.

- An ignition interlock device placed on your vehicle. You will have this device for the duration of your hardship license and once the hardship hours are removed, you will be required to have the device for an additional 2 years on the full time license.

- A lifetime loss of your CDL, if you have one.

A common alternative offered in many 2nd OUI cases includes the following terms:

- A guilty finding with 2 years' probation and a suspended jail sentence. You will not be required to go to jail unless you violate the terms of your probation.

- 14-day inpatient treatment program and a 26 week outpatient aftercare program, which you pay for (approximately $1,000).

- A 2 year license suspension, but you may be eligible for a work/education hardship exemption in 1 year. This is in addition to any other suspension you face. (See above as it relates to the calculation of the hardship license.)

- An ignition interlock device placed on your vehicle. You will have this device for the duration of your hardship license; and once the hardship hours are removed, you will be required to have the device for an additional 2 years on the full time license.

Massachusetts has a "lifetime lookback" rule. In other words, previous OUIs on your record do not "expire," no matter where or when they occurred.

Third Offense

A third OUI offense in Massachusetts comes with penalties like:

- $1,000 to $15,000 in fines,

- 150 days (150 days is a minimum mandatory sentence) to 2 ½ years (30 months) in prison,

- 8 year driver's license suspension,

- Ignition interlock device required on your vehicle.

If you refused to take a breath test, your license will be suspended for 5 years. If you took the breath test and blew a .08 or above, your license will be suspended for 30 days.

Penalties that are commonly imposed on those convicted of a third OUI in Massachusetts include:

- A felony conviction on their record,

- A jail sentence of 150 days (minimum) to 5 years (maximum) in state prison,

- A suspended sentence with probation. If you violate probation, the judge can send you back to prison to finish serving the sentence.

- A fine of $1,000 to $15,000,

- 8 year license suspension, with exemptions considered at 2 years and 4 years. This is in addition to any other suspension you face. It is important to note that the 8 year suspension is consecutive to the 5 year refusal suspension. You have to serve 2 year of the 8 years suspension. Essentially, you will not be eligible for a hardship license through the RMV for 7 years, although you may apply to the Board of Appeals sooner to request hardship relief. This gets confusing, so make sure you have a lawyer who can clearly communicate your license options and eligibility for a hardship license.

- An ignition interlock device installed on your vehicle. You will have this device for the duration of your hardship license; and once the hardship hours are removed, you will be required to have the device for an additional 2 years on the full time license.

A third OUI offense in Massachusetts is a felony. Like a first or second misdemeanor OUI, however, if you fight the charges and win, no conviction appears on your record. If you lose at trial or you plead guilty, the conviction does appear on your record.

Fourth Offense

Like a third offense, a fourth OUI offense in Massachusetts is a felony. Again, the penalties for this offense escalate. They include:

- $1,500 to $25,000 in fines,

- 1 to 3 years (12 to 36 months) in prison (1 year minimum mandatory sentence) or up to 5 years if indicted in Superior Court.

- 10 year license suspension, with exemptions considered at 5 years and 8 years. If you refused a breath test, however, your license will be suspended for life.

- Ignition interlock device required on your vehicle.

- A felony conviction on your record.

If you refused to take the breath test on a fourth offense, your driver's license will be suspended for life. If you took the breath test and blew a .08 or above, your driver's license will be suspended for 30 days.

Occasionally, a person faces a fifth OUI offense charge in Massachusetts. Penalties for these charges are similar to those for a fourth offense, except that the minimum mandatory jail sentence increases to 2 years, minimum fines increase to $2,000, and there is no possibility for a return of your driver's license – it is automatically suspended for life, whether or not you agreed to the breath test.

Why should I fight the charges?

In most cases, the penalties you face if you go to court and lose are not much different than the penalties you face if you plead guilty. Going to court, however, opens up the chance that you might win –

meaning that the OUI won't appear on your record at all.

OUI cases are not always "open and shut." They rely heavily on a mix of scientific evidence, pseudo-scientific observations requiring balance and coordination under extremely stressful circumstances. Massachusetts law gives judges leeway to determine how heavily scientific data should be weighed in court, which gives your lawyer the opportunity to point out the pitfalls in relying on much commonly-used OUI evidence. For instance, the horizontal gaze nystagmus test, which is commonly given by law enforcement, is commonly excluded because the police officers/troopers are not qualified as experts to talk about the test.

Evidence Commonly Used in OUI Cases (and Its Pitfalls)

In any OUI case, the prosecution must prove that you were, in fact, operating a motor vehicle "under the influence" of alcohol or other substances. To do this, police and prosecutors typically focus on three types of evidence:

- Your driving behavior,

- Your performance on field sobriety tests,

- The results of a breath test, if any, and

- The results of a blood test, if any.

Each of these can be addressed by an experienced lawyer. Here are some of the arguments that may be used in your case to challenge the evidence and create reasonable doubt.

Field Sobriety Testing

Despite what police and prosecutors say, there is nothing "scientific" about field sobriety tests (FSTs). Instead, they rely solely on what an officer thinks he or she sees while you perform them – and medical issues, weather, road conditions, and even your choice of shoes can affect your performance.

There are many types of field sobriety tests. Most police forces today rely on three standardized tests:

the horizontal gaze nystagmus (HGN) test, the "walk and turn" test, and the "one-leg stand."

Here are some of the biggest known problems with each of these three tests:

- **Horizontal Gaze Nystagmus:** The HGN test has been called into serious question in nearly every state. It uses a penlight or other object to track someone's eye movements, on the theory that intoxication causes nystagmus, or jerking of the eye, more readily. While nystagmus can be evaluated by a qualified medical professional, police do not have the medical training required to interpret the results accurately – leading to this test being routinely excluded in Massachusetts courts when it is contested.

- **Walk and Turn:** Officers are taught to judge everyone who takes this test according to the same standard, whether they are young or old, fit or out of shape, able-bodied or disabled. The standards are exacting, and every real or perceived "mistake" is used against the test-taker. The bottom line is that your inability to perform this test has no correlation to your ability to drive a car.

- **One-Leg Stand.** Another test of balance and coordination that is given to everyone and judged the same for everyone, no matter their state of health or ability. In some cases, people are actually required to take these tests in shoes that make them nearly impossible – like high heels or flip-flop sandals.

A good OUI lawyer has the ability to effectively examine the officer/trooper to show various aspects of the exercises that the client performed well or in accordance with the instructions, thus the exercises become ambiguous to any jury or judge. Challenging the results of FSTs is not difficult if you have an OUI lawyer who is prepared and who can show that performance on these tests has nothing to do with whether you were impaired from alcohol.

Often times, a client will be charged with Operating under the Inlfuence of Drugs, and your client was examined at the police station by a police officer/ trooper who is a Drug Recognition Expert, or DRE.

The goal of DRE is to examine a person to determine three things:

- Is this person impaired to the extent we'd expect, when compared with their BAC score?

- Is the impairment due to drugs, or due to a medical impairment?

- If the impairment is due to drugs, which category of drugs is it most likely to be?

The DRE training is more extensive than the basic OUI training all police officers and troopers receive in the academy. DRE training is run by the International Association of Chiefs of Police (IACP), and it requires two days of training, practice evaluations, rigorous "passing" score requirements, and endorsement by two certified DREs. These requirements make DRE training sound tough – and make it sound scientific and reliable. As a result, DREs are frequently offered in OUI Drug cases as "expert witnesses."

In fact, DRE can successfully be challenged in court. Massachusetts courts examine expert witnesses according to the *Daubert-Lanigan* standard (named after the two cases that established it, *Daubert v. Merrell Dow Pharms., Inc.* (1993) and *Commonwealth v. Lanigan* (1994)).

The Daubert-Lanigan standard demands that the party that wants to use an "expert witness" is responsible for proving that the expert's science is "reliable." The reliability of the expert's scientific method has to be proven "by a preponderance of proof." In other words, it has to be "more likely than not" that the expert's scientific method is reliable. Error rates, personal observation, straying from the manual, and other errors in the process can all call into question a DRE's scientific reliability.

Breath and Blood Testing

Both breath and blood tests seek to establish a person's blood alcohol concentration (BAC). However, the rules for each test are different in Massachusetts.

When it comes to **breath testing**, Massachusetts is an "implied consent" state. In other words, you are held to have agreed to breath testing when you accepted your driver's license. Refusing a breath test comes with additional penalties – usually a much longer suspension of your driver's license.

Although they are commonly used, breath tests are not infallible. For instance, readings can be inconsistent. Also, the readings are usually only accurate to the second decimal place – so while a reading of .07 might be accurate, a reading of .079 might not.

Defense lawyers frequently challenge breath test readings under the rule laid down in *Commonwealth v. Zeininger*, 459 Mass. 775 (2011), or by examining whether the officers/trooper followed the regulations in administering the test. (501 CMR 2.01 et seq.)

Blood tests are different. Generally speaking, if the police want a blood draw, one of two things must happen:

- You have to be under arrest and consent to the blood draw, or

- The police have to have a warrant to draw your blood.

Once the blood is taken, it may pass through several people's hands before it is finally tested. The test, which is often performed on a gas chromatograph, must be performed correctly on a fully functional, calibrated machine in order to produce accurate results. Your lawyer can get the information needed to show where any problems in this process occurred.

If you were in an accident or injured, your blood may be drawn at the hospital as part of the treatment you received. The prosecution may file a motion to obtain these medical records – but it has to show that the records are "relevant" to your case under *Commonwealth v. Lampron,* 65 Mass. App. Ct. 340

(2005). Your lawyer can oppose this motion. If the opposition succeeds, you keep the blood test results out of court.

Even if a hospital blood draw comes in, there are known problems with the method. For instance, it is usually a serum test, not a whole blood test; an expert will be required to test the sample. Also, there is rarely a calibration or a "back up" check for reliability and accuracy. In other words, if the hospital's test is wrong, there is simply no way to know – and thus no way to know if it is right.

Insurance and Licenses: Can I Get Back on the Road After My OUI?

An arrest for OUI in Massachusetts comes with a license suspension in most cases. If you are convicted, you also face license suspension or revocation. How many OUI offenses you have on your record will control how long you will need to wait to get a hardship license. Because the RMV has tightened up the process for getting an exemption, however, it's important to work with a lawyer to maximize your chances of qualifying.

Another alternative is to work with your lawyer to argue for a shorter license suspension. For instance, your lawyer may be able to argue for a 45 to 90-day suspension if this was your first offense, and you enrolled in an alcohol education program. If you are under 21, the minimum license suspension is 210 days, but you can still be eligible for a hardship license.

Are there any restrictions on my license if I get an exemption?

If you receive a hardship exemption, your license will still be restricted in some ways. You will be limited to driving only in a certain 12-hour period every day, seven days per week. This window can be set to allow you to go to work or school. It is called a work license, but once it is issued, the license can be used for any purpose.

You will also be required to have an ignition interlock device installed, unless this is your first OUI.

What about an ignition interlock device?

An ignition interlock device (IID) is installed in your vehicle at your expense. It requires you to give a breath sample, which the device analyzes for alcohol. If alcohol is detected, the vehicle will not start.

Massachusetts requires drivers who have received a second, third, or fourth OUI to have an IID installed once they begin driving again – even if they are doing so under an exemption.

Insurance After an OUI

Dealing with license revocations, ignition inter-lock devices, and court fees aren't the only costs you might face after an OUI. The cost of your auto insurance may also increase – if your insurance carrier agrees to keep covering your vehicle at all.

When you insure your vehicle after an OUI, pay attention to RMV requirements. Massachusetts does not require what is commonly referred to as an SR-22. (The "SR" stands for "safety responsibility.")

Getting Your Life Back in Order After Your OUI Defense

*"Being challenged in
life is inevitable. Being
defeated is optional."*

– Roger Crawford

In this section, we'll look at the non-legal issues that may affect your life after an OUI arrest, charge, or conviction. We'll tackle questions like:

- How can I avoid losing my job or getting kicked out of school?

- What if I can't avoid that?

- How do I tell people about my OUI or the restrictions my sentence puts on me?

- How do I get errands done if I can't drive?

- Do I have an alcohol or drug problem? If so, what can I do about it?

The goal of this section is to help you overcome the obstacles you face, learn from your mistakes, and avoid trouble in the future. By applying these tips, you can turn your OUI into an opportunity for personal growth and redemption. This event in your life does not define you as a person!!

Maintaining Your Ties to Work and School

One of the first things most people worry about is whether their OUI will affect their work, their schooling, or both. This is a legitimate concern. It is important to take steps to demonstrate that you care about your work and that you intend to learn from this experience and move forward.

Can I be fired for a DUI?

Massachusetts is an "at-will" employment state. In other words, unless you have a contract that specifically states otherwise, an employer may fire you for any reason or no reason at all. This includes an OUI.

However, whether or not you *will* lose your job depends on a number of factors, such as:

- **What kind of job is it?** For instance, if your job requires a CDL and you no longer have one due to your conviction, you will lose your current job because you can no longer carry it out.

- **What is the company's policy for criminal convictions?** Some company policies require termination of anyone who is convicted or admits to any crime. Others focus only on felonies or on certain types of crime, like fraud, theft, or violence.

- **What does your contract say?** If you have a contract, its provisions for how to treat workers convicted of crimes will govern what happens on the job.

You can take active steps to help yourself avoid being fired over an OUI. For instance:

- **Fight the charges.** Work with a board-certified OUI defense attorney to fight the charges and challenge your license suspension.

- **Talk to your boss about alternate work.** If your OUI or license suspension prevents you from doing your current job, ask to be assigned to work that doesn't require you to drive. Or ask to share tasks with co-workers, so that they do your driving and you do their non-driving work.

- **Be ready to talk about what you bring to the company.** An OUI can loom large in a manager's mind, making it hard for them to remember what you've given to the company over the years. Be ready to talk about what you've accomplished and how you've gone "above and beyond" – and how important it is to you not to let this one mistake stand in the way of helping your co-workers.

Can I be kicked out of school?

Colleges and universities operate on different rules than employers – but many have policies that may result in you being suspended, expelled, or kicked out of your current program of study for an OUI.

To manage the potential consequences of an OUI on your schooling, look at the following factors:

- **How does an OUI get reported to the school?** Many colleges and universities receive reports when students are convicted of a crime. Find out whether your school does, who gets those reports, and what happens to them. This will tell you who to talk to and what to prepare for.

- **What does my program of study require?** Talk to your advisor or to the dean of your college. If you are in training for a job that requires a license, like nursing or teaching, you may be barred from finishing or be unable to get a job when you do. If this happens, consider another path.

- **What about my financial aid?** Check your scholarship and loan paperwork. Some financial aid policies state that the aid will be revoked if you are convicted of a crime.

- **How can my lawyer help?** Your attorney may be able to help represent you if the school decides to expel or suspend you. Talk to your lawyer about your options in this situation.

If you lose your driving privileges or must spend time in jail or a treatment program, be proactive: talk to your advisor about your options for taking a semester off, studying online, or finding alternate ways to finish your tasks.

What if I Can't Avoid Being Fired or Kicked Out of School?

Despite your best efforts, you may not be able to prevent your employer or school from sending you away. If this happens, keep these tips in mind:

1. Focus on the future.

It's easy to get bogged down in feelings of anger, resentment, or regret. While it is important to process these feelings, don't let them make your future decisions for you. Instead, start looking for your next job or education opportunity.

2. Be ready to fight for unemployment insurance.

If you were fired from your job, you may decide to file for unemployment. But be ready for a challenge from your employer. Generally speaking, you are not entitled to unemployment if your employer can show that you broke a reasonable, uniformly-applied rule – such as a rule stated in your employee handbook against receiving a criminal conviction.

Your lawyer can help you fight for unemployment or find an attorney with experience in this specific area.

3. Read the fine print.

When applying for new jobs or to attend another school, read the application materials carefully. If your OUI was a misdemeanor conviction, you do not have to disclose it on the form if the form asks if you've been convicted of a felony. If it asks about any criminal conviction, however, you do have to disclose it.

4. Be ready to talk about what you've learned.

Your OUI may come up during a job interview or school application process. If it does, be ready. Prepare an answer that shows that you know you made a mistake, and that lists the steps you are taking to make sure you do not make that mistake again.

How to Talk About Your OUI or the Penalties You Face

In your job, at school, or in other activities in your life, you may need to talk about your OUI conviction or the things you can and cannot do because of probation, a restricted license, or other penalties you face.

These conversations can be tough to have. But you can prepare for them. Here's how:

1. Keep it "need to know."
Before mentioning your OUI, probation, or any other fact related to your case, ask: Why does this person need to know?

Your employer may need to know if you cannot do part of your job because you can't drive. A prospective employer may need to know if the application asks "Have you ever been convicted and/or charged with any crime?" Your child's babysitter may need to know if you can no longer drive your child to daycare.

2. Only tell what the other person needs to know.
When talking about your situation, stick only to the facts the other party needs. You don't always have to explain that your problem is due to your OUI conviction – but sometimes, you do.

For example, if your job requires you to report a criminal conviction, state only that you are reporting a conviction for OUI, and mention the rule or policy that requires you to report it.

If you are explaining to the babysitter that you are late picking up your child because you had to take the bus, however, there's no need to say that you have to take the bus because of your license suspension. Simply say, "I'm sorry I'm late. I had to take the bus."

3. Stick to the facts and the future.

If you are asked about your OUI, or if you want to explain your situation to someone whose opinion matters to you:

- Stick to the **facts.** Trying to place blame or explain your actions is more likely to confuse your audience than anything. Instead, focus on what happened: "I was charged with a drunk driving charge or convicted of driving drunk last month. Because of that, I can't drive for a while."

- Focus on the **future.** Talk about what you learned and what you are doing (or want to do) to minimize the impact of your sentence on the other person. For example, "My lawyer and I are seeking a work license, which would allow me to start driving sooner. In the meantime, my kids will take the bus to school, and I was hoping you'd let me tag along on your Saturday grocery run."

If you want, you can also talk about what you learned from the experience. "I haven't driven under the influence since the accident. Next time, if I think I'm going to be driving, I'm just not going to drink."

4. Find a confidante you trust.
While the tips above are the best way to talk to co-workers, friends, and acquaintances about your situation, you'll also need someone you can rely on to listen to your fears, help you process your feelings, and provide solid advice. Your spouse or a close family member may be able to do this, or you may wish to work with a licensed therapist. (See "What to Do About It" below.)

"Life Hacks" for Tackling Your To-Do List Despite Your Restricted License

Your responsibilities don't vanish just because your driver's license has been revoked, suspended, or restricted. You still need to get to work, run errands, and meet your family's needs – and you need to do it without the risk of being arrested for driving with a suspended license.

Here are some ways to take care of your responsibilities without getting behind the wheel yourself:

1. Team up with friends.

Ask friends and family members if you can tag along on their weekly errand trips to the grocery store, sporting events, and other places. See if your children can carpool with their friends to school, sports, and other events. Often, those who love you will be willing to help you take care of your family.

2. Look into delivery services.

Most major U.S. cities have multiple services that deliver groceries. Amazon Prime ships many food items nationwide, and the company has also started offering full-service grocery delivery services in the Boston area. Services like Instacart, FreshDirect, and Peapod will also ship food.

But the convenience of delivery doesn't end with groceries. Many localities have companies that will also pick up and drop off laundry. Also, check all the websites for your local businesses and your bank – most have web or smartphone apps that will let you do everything from refilling prescriptions to depositing checks without having to appear in person.

3. Try Uber, Lyft, or public transportation.

Some U.S. cities have workable public transportation. Others are a public transport "dead zone." Start by checking out the local bus, train, or subway schedules. Compare them to your own schedule to see if taking public transport is workable. If the bus goes right past your workplace but will drop you off half an hour early, is there a coffee shop, library, or park in which you can spend your time until work opens?

If public transport isn't an option, ride-sharing services like Uber and Lyft can offer a cost-conscious alternative to taxi services. These companies also frequently offer free-ride specials to new subscribers. With technology being so advanced, some clients have found themselves to be more productive and efficient in getting tasks done while being transported to personal or work related events and some continued to use the alternative transportation options even after their license has been reinstated.

4. Ask about flex time, telecommuting, or online classes.

If your transportation options make it hard to get to work or school on time, ask your employer about flex time or telecommuting options. For students, look into online classes. Flex time lets you shift the start or end of your workday – so you can start working an hour early if that's when the bus drops you off, or you can plan to leave work in time to walk your kids from school to soccer practice. Telecommuting and online education both let you do your work from anyplace in the world with an Internet connection, instantly solving the problem of finding reliable transportation to work or school.

Being left without the ability to drive requires you to get creative. Nevertheless, nearly all of us have been stranded without a car at least once due to breakdowns, bad weather, or other life events. Don't hesitate to ask how friends or co-workers solved the problem of being without wheels.

How to Know if You Have a Problem – And What to Do About It

---

*"Life's challenges are not supposed
to paralyze you. They're supposed
to help you discover who you are."*

– Bernice Johnson Reagon

Did you just make one mistake on a night of careless fun? Or do you have a drinking problem?

This question haunts many people after their first OUI conviction. After a second or third conviction, the question becomes even more pressing.

Do I have a problem with alcohol?

Every person who has ever struggled to control their drinking or drug use has found the answer to this question in a different way. Some are ready to believe a "yes" answer immediately; others struggle for years to deny or control the problem, and may run into trouble many times before finally accepting the truth.

To explore this possibility, consider these five questions. You may also want to have a family member or close friend answer them as well:

1. **Do I get a physical craving for alcohol before I drink or once I start drinking?** Are you unable to "shut it off" once you start?

2. **Do I obsess about drinking?** Are you preoccupied with alcohol-related thoughts, such as "How much is left in the house?", "Where I can pick up more?", or "Can I get a drink at the party?"

3. **Have I compromised my morals or values due to drinking?** This might happen either while you are drinking, or as part of an attempt to put alcohol above other things. Most people who have been convicted of an OUI put their OUI in this category.

4. **How often do I repeat these patterns, either willingly or unwillingly?** How often have the three things above occurred in the past few months or years?

5. **Can I imagine life without alcohol?** If being prohibited from drinking was one of the hardest parts of facing your OUI conviction, you may have a problem.

6. **Has alcohol affected your family relationships with your wife, children or other family members?** Does alcohol affect your work performance? Are you showing up to work frequently with a "hang over"?

Additional resources like those on the National Council on Alcoholism and Drug Dependence (NCADD) website can also help. One option NCADD offers is its "Am I Alcoholic?" self-test. The test consists of 26 yes or no questions, and it is scored instantly with a click of the "next" button.

I think I have a problem. What can I do?

Addiction is a complex set of behaviors. Studies indicate that addiction is not as simple as mere physical dependence on a substance. If you believe you have a drinking problem, you will probably need to take several different steps together to address the different "sides" of the behavior.

Some steps that have worked for many people include:

1. Committing to stop drinking.

This step is at the core of all successful recovery from alcoholism – but it is also the hardest step to make. Very few people succeed at simply going "cold turkey." Instead, they make gradual changes with support from other sources that allow them to step away and to stay away. Nevertheless, this is the commitment you will need to return to every time you feel yourself waver.

2. Make a cost-benefit table.
A cost-benefit table can help you compare the costs and benefits of drinking in an objective, non-judgmental way. Take a piece of paper and divide it into four sections, with labels:

	Drinking	Not Drinking
Benefits		
Costs		

Then, fill in the squares:

	Drinking	**Not Drinking**
Benefits	Helps me forget about my problems. It's fun. It helps me relax.	My relationships would probably get better. I'd feel better. No more waking up feeling gross. I'd have more time and energy for the people I love.
Costs	I got an OUI. I feel ashamed of it. Sometimes I can't do my job or watch the kids because of it.	I'd have to relax and have fun some other way. My drinking buddies wouldn't stick around. I'd have to deal with my problems.

The items that go in each square will be different for each person. Nonetheless, this chart can help you "untangle" fact from feeling, so you can make a clear choice.

3. Set clear goals.

Setting clear goals related to your drinking and related problems can help you change your behavior and be proud of your progress. Set goals that are SMART: **S**pecific, **M**easurable, **A**chievable, **R**ealistic, and **T**ime-Bound.

For example, compare these two goals:

1. I will drink less.

2. Starting this weekend, I will drink no more than two drinks per day on Saturday and Sunday, and no drinking at all during the week.

The first goal is vague. It's also tough to measure. What does "drink less" look like? How will you know when you have reached your goal to "drink less"? How long do you have to get there?

The second goal is a SMART goal. It's specific as to what "drink less" looks like, how you will do it, and when you will get there. It's measurable: you can tell if you've had only two drinks on Saturday or if you had three. If it's a goal you think you can do, it's achievable and realistic. And it's time-specific: you know when you will start, which days are "open" for drinking, and which are not.

3. Build your internal and external support networks.

To meet this goal (or any big goal), you'll need the support of others. You'll also need to support yourself. Here's where to start:

- **Improve your self-care steps.** Consider setting SMART goals focused on eating well, exercising, and getting plenty of sleep. Healthier living will help you combat mood swings and cravings, and it'll give you a project to focus on.

- **Build a Team You.** Seek out the people who support your positive, healthy changes and who help you feel good about yourself – without drinking. Investing in people and your community will help you stay motivated.

- **Get a new hobby or interest.** Hobbies, projects, and volunteer activities can all give you something to live for, which makes drinking less appealing.

- **Learn to manage stress.** Learning to recognize and manage your stress levels is one of the most empowering steps you can take. Exercise, meditation, journaling, breathing exercises, and progressive relaxation techniques can all put you in charge of the "stress monster."

- **Seek treatment.** Therapy, support groups like Alcoholics Anonymous, and other sources can help you deal with particularly tough spots in your recovery and stay on track. Check out the "Resources" section in this guidebook for help.

While this list is intended to provide a starting point, it is not comprehensive. The right combination of supports for each person is unique to that individual. It's important to seek out a therapist or other licensed professional who can help, especially if you have trouble making changes "stick" on your own.

Massachusetts OUI Resources

"There are no secrets to success. It is the result of preparation, hard work, and learning from failure."

— Colin Powell

After an OUI, you need information and resources to help you get your life back together. Here are several sources you can use to find a therapist, work through addiction, find a treatment program, and more.

OUI Defense Videos

Want to know more about what happens if you are arrested or charged with OUI in Massachusetts? This series of educational videos focuses on specific points in the process, including OUI charges, the penalties for 1st and 2nd OUIs, the 24D program for alcohol education, and how a Continuance Without a Finding (CWOF) may be used in some OUI cases.

http://www.massachusetts-drunkdriving.com

National Institutes of Health – Understanding Drug Abuse & Addiction

The National Institute on Drug Abuse, part of the National Institutes of Health, publishes a free guide titled *Understanding Drug Abuse and Addiction: What the Science Says*. The entire guide is available online. The NIDA also offers other guides in the same series, including *Principles of Substance Abuse Prevention* and *Drugs, Brains, and Behavior: The Science of Addiction*. These guides provide a scientifically-based understanding of addiction and offer guidance for treating it successfully.

https://www.drugabuse.gov/publications/teaching-packets/understanding-drug-abuse-addiction/section-i

Massachusetts Health and Human Services – Search for Substance Abuse Services

The Massachusetts Department of Health and Human Services maintains a directory of treatment programs that are funded and licensed by the Bureau of Substance Abuse Services (BSAS). You can search by region and by program type (including prevention, residential treatment, ambulatory services, aftercare, and homeless services) to find exactly the support you need. The entire Directory can also be downloaded for free in PDF format.

http://db.state.ma.us/dph/bsas/search.asp

DUI Alcohol Education Programs

This comprehensive table of BSAS-approved providers for DUI offender programs in Massachusetts can help you find an alcohol education program that meets the requirements for programs for first or second offense OUI convictions in Massachusetts. If your probation requires you to seek treatment, this table can help you find the nearest program that meets your needs.

http://www.massachusetts-drunkdriving.com/
dui-alcohol-education-programs-in-massachusetts/

National Institute on Alcohol Abuse and Alcoholism: Treatment for Alcohol Problems

The National Institute on Alcohol Abuse and Alcoholism (NIAAA), part of the National Institutes of Health, publishes a free guide titled "Treatment for Alcohol Problems: Finding and Getting Help." The entire guide is available online. Topics covered in the guide include "When Is It Time for Treatment?", "Options for Treatment," and "Tips for Selecting Treatment." It covers both self-guided treatment and treatments led by health professionals, including medication options.

http://pubs.niaaa.nih.gov/publications/Treatment/
treatment.htm

HelpGuide: Alcohol Abuse Treatment and Self-Help

HelpGuide offers a comprehensive how-to guide on examining your own behavior, setting goals, and taking steps to change unhealthy behaviors into healthy ones. While not a substitute for qualified medical advice, the guide can help you break down your everyday actions to determine what needs to change and where you should start asking professionals for help.

http://www.helpguide.org/articles/addiction/alcohol-addiction-treatment-and-self-help.htm

Groups for Families and Friends

Recovery from alcohol or drug abuse is a group effort. Families and friends need to know how to support their loved one in healthy ways, and they also need a safe place to discuss their own fears and concerns. Resources like Al-Anon Family Groups or Adult Children of Alcoholics can help.

Al-Anon Family Groups: http://www.al-anon.alateen.org, or call toll-free 1-888-425-2666 for meetings.

Adult Children of Alcoholics: http://www.adult-children.org, or call 310-534-1815.

Massachusetts Behavioral Health Partnership: Find a Behavioral Health Provider

Behavioral health providers focus on helping people change problematic or dangerous behaviors to develop a new, healthier approach to life. The MBHP database allows you to search for a behavioral health provider by name, location, focus area, and languages spoken.

https://www.masspartnership.com/member/FindBHProvider.aspx

Network Therapy: Find a Therapist in Massachusetts

Network Therapy's therapist database allows you to search by city or by ZIP code. It also lists treatment centers, support groups, and national hotlines for a wide range of conditions and concerns. In addition, its informational network allows you to research conditions and medications before making the right treatment decision for you.

http://www.networktherapy.com/directory/therapist_index.asp?state=MA

Psychology Today: Find a Therapist

Psychology Today, the popular psychology magazine, also maintains a large online database of therapists in a wide range of disciplines and practice areas. Search by state, county, or city to discover who is available in your area and where they focus their work.

https://therapists.psychologytoday.com/rms/state/Massachusetts.html

Books and Guides

Dr. Lance Dodes focuses on identifying and treating addiction using the most up to date scientific understandings of addiction behaviors. His books include *The Heart of Addiction: A New Approach to Understanding and Managing Alcoholism and Other Addictive Behaviors, Breaking Addiction: A 7-Step Handbook for Ending any Addiction,* and *The Sober*

Truth: Debunking the Bad Science Behind 12-Step Programs and the Rehab Industry.

http://www.lancedodes.com/purchase-my-books-tod/

Amazon.com, Goodreads, and other online book sites maintain regular best-seller and highest-rated lists of books on substance abuse recovery. Current titles on the Amazon list include Melody Beattie's *Codependent No More* and Maia Szalavitz's *Unbroken Brain: A Revolutionary New Way of Understanding Addiction.*

http://www.amazon.com/Best-Sellers-Books-Substance-Abuse-Recovery/zgbs/books/4725

Conclusion

*"It's hard to beat a person
who never gives up."*

— *Babe Ruth*

While the data show that many Americans drink
and drive regularly, it also indicates that those who
get caught do so because they made a serious mistake in the wrong place at the wrong time.

An arrest or charge for OUI can greatly complicate
your life; a conviction can have long-lasting consequences. You may find yourself struggling to get
to work or school, make sure your kids get to the
places they need to go, or run even basic errands.
Friends may decide they don't want to talk to you;
your boss may restrict your work – or worse, fire you
altogether.

On top of this, the experience of an OUI can have you questioning your own behavior. Do you really have an alcohol problem? Was your driving that unsafe? How can you avoid ever having to go through a nightmare like this again?

The good news is that you *can* put your life back together after an OUI. Fighting the charges allows you to protect your legal rights and gives you a chance of being found not guilty, keeping the incident off your record – and the penalties if you lose are not much higher than if you plead guilty. If you are convicted, you can take steps to protect your job and meet your responsibilities. And if you do suspect you have a problem, a wide range of treatment options can help you address it from every possible angle, maximizing your chances of improving your life and avoiding a future OUI charge.

This handbook is intended as a starting point to familiarize you with the process of an OUI. For help fighting an OUI charge or getting your life back on track after a conviction, seek advice from the right professionals. A qualified therapist can help you succeed at recovery – and an experienced, board-certified OUI defense lawyer in Massachusetts can help you fight the charges and protect your legal rights. For more information, please call our offices at **(888) OUI-ATTY (684-6494)** for a free and confidential case evaluation.

LAW OFFICE OF
James M. Milligan, Jr.

Contact us
James M. Milligan
Board Certified DUI Defense
308 Washington Street,
Norwell, Massachusetts 02061

Phone: 888-684-6494

www.Massachusetts-DrunkDriving.com

Disclaimer for "The Massachusetts OUI Survival Guide: A Step-by-Step Guide to Defending Against Your Charges and Getting Your Life Back"

You understand that this book is not intended as a substitution for a consultation with an attorney. Requesting this book or viewing the information in it does not create an attorney-client relationship with The Law Office of James M. Milligan or any of its attorneys. To obtain legal advice, please engage the services of Law Office of James M. Milligan or another law firm of your choice. To discuss engaging Law Office of James M. Milligan to help you with your DUI, please contact the firm.

LAW OFFICE OF JAMES M. MILLIGAN IS PROVIDING " THE MASSACHUSETTS

OUI SURVIVAL GUIDE: A STEP-BY-STEP GUIDE TO DEFENDING AGAINST YOUR CHARGES AND GETTING YOUR LIFE BACK" (HEREAFTER REFERRED TO AS "BOOK") AND ITS CONTENTS ON AN "AS IS" BASIS AND MAKES NO REPRESENTATIONS OR WARRANTIES OF ANY KIND WITH RESPECT TO THIS BOOK OR ITS CONTENTS. LAW OFFICE OF JAMES M. MILLIGAN DISCLAIMS ALL SUCH REPRESENTATIONS AND WARRANTIES, INCLUDING FOR EXAMPLE WARRANTIES OF |MERCHANTABILITY AND FITNESS FOR A PARTICULAR PURPOSE. IN ADDITION, LAW OFFICE OF JAMES M. MILLIGAN DOES NOT REPRESENT OR WARRANT THAT THE INFORMATION ACCESSIBLE VIA THIS BOOK IS ACCURATE, COMPLETE OR CURRENT.

Except as specifically stated in this book, neither Law Office of James M. Milligan nor any authors, contributors, or other representatives will be liable for damages arising out of or in connection with the use of this book. This is a comprehensive limitation of liability that applies to all damages of any kind, including (without limitation) compensatory; direct, indirect or consequential damages; loss of data, income or profit; loss of or damage to property and claims of third parties.

You hereby release Law Office of James M. Milligan and the publisher from any liability related to this book to the fullest extent permitted by law. This includes any damages, costs, or losses of any nature arising from the use of this book and the information provided by this book, including direct, consequential, special, punitive, or incidental damages, even if Law Office of James M. Milligan has been advised of the possibility of such damages.